GRATITUDE JOURNAL: DAILY CHECK-IN

GRATITUDE JOURNAL

JOURNAL

DAILY CHECK-IN

60 Days of Reflection Space
to Track, Support, and
Appreciate the Good in Life

ROCKRIDGE
PRESS

First Rockridge Press trade paperback edition 2022

Rockridge Press and the Rockridge Press logo are trademarks or registered trademarks of Callisto Media Inc. and/or its affiliates in the United States and other countries and may not be used without written permission.

For general information on our other products and services, please contact our Customer Care Department within the United States at (866) 744-2665, or outside the United States at (510) 253-0500.

Some of the activities originally appeared, in different form, in *The Five-Minute Gratitude Journal: Give Thanks, Practice Positivity, Find Joy*; *A Year of Gratitude Journal: 52 Weeks of Prompts and Exercises to Cultivate Positivity and Joy*; *A Year of Gratitude: Daily Moments of Reflection, Grace, and Thanks*; *The Daily Gratitude Journal for Men: 90 Days of Mindfulness and Reflection*; and *Self-Care Journal: Daily Check-In*.

Paperback ISBN: 979-8-88650-087-5

Manufactured in the United States of America

Interior and Cover Designer: Jake Flaherty
Art Producer: Samantha Ulban
Editor: Rachelle Cihonski
Production Editor: Jenna Dutton
Production Manager: Riley Hoffman

All images courtesy of © Shutterstock

10 9 8 7 6 5 4 3 2 1 0

This journal belongs to:

CONTENTS

INTRODUCTION

People often wonder, "What is the secret to happiness?" The answer is gratitude.

Gratitude is the feeling of appreciation we have for the people, experiences, and things in our lives that have helped or supported us in some way. You may notice that the more dissatisfied or unappreciative you feel, the more difficult it is to access positive emotions. Gratitude is a powerful tool unlike any other, one that scientists and spiritual teachers alike report to have the greatest happiness-boosting benefits.

When practiced occasionally, gratitude has a noticeable impact on our day-to-day lives; when practiced consistently, it can transform our lives for the better in remarkable ways that we couldn't have imagined. You know you've encountered gratitude when you feel alive, joyful, and satisfied with your life just as it is in the moment. You know you've been cultivating gratitude for some time when you feel personally more resilient, content, and optimistic, and all-around more compassionate, kind, and connected to others.

Despite what you might've heard before, gratitude is not an attitude—it's a practice. This journal is your most powerful tool for making this practice part of your life. It is said that all good habits start small. If so, journaling about gratitude is the perfect way to turn gratitude from an occasional occurrence into a consistent practice. The more you do it, the more it becomes

a habit. The more it becomes a habit, the easier it becomes for you to do it every day.

Maybe this journal was gifted to you. Maybe you went out and found it on your own. However it ended up in your hands, if you make a habit of using this journal, you'll come out of this sixty-day journey as a more centered, more fulfilled, and more successful version of yourself.

HOW TO USE
THIS JOURNAL

This journal will guide you in learning more about your relationship to gratitude. You will keep tabs on your daily rituals, moods, energy levels, goals, and intentions to reflect on your gratitude. You will answer thought-provoking questions that will help you gain insight into your specific needs. You will also be provided with exercises and tips to aid you on your gratitude journey.

Try to use each part of this journal to help you identify the routines and rituals that are beneficial to you, the ones that are not helpful, and the ones that are life-changing, so you can build a gratitude practice that is right for you. Remember, you can modify and change your gratitude routine at any time. In fact, you are encouraged to do so on this journey, as it is highly likely that your needs will change as your life does. Also, what works for another person may not work for you, so don't be afraid to modify common gratitude practices to meet your own needs—flexibility is key.

Part 1 of this journal will provide you with an introduction to gratitude, including foundational information you'll need before diving into your practice. In part 2, you will find sixty days of trackers, prompts, tips, and exercises to help you build, track, and expand on your gratitude and reach your goals. Each entry

has been thoughtfully designed to transport you into a state of gratitude. Simply open your journal, fill in the date, and begin writing. Before you know it, you'll feel lighter, happier, and more optimistic. After sixty days of consistent practice, grateful won't just be something that you want to be—it will be something you *are*!

Congratulations on taking the first step toward becoming a more grateful you. Whatever your personal goals, individual desires, and reasons for wanting to foster an attitude of gratitude, this journal is here to help you on your way. You know what life can be like without a consistent practice of gratitude, so why not see what life can be like with one?

PART ONE

UNDERSTANDING GRATITUDE

There is so much gratitude to be found in small, everyday moments. The more mindful we are of the little things, the more we're able to harness that thankful energy and extend it into all aspects of our life. Before you dive into your sixty-day gratitude journaling journey in part 2, part 1 of this journal will provide some foundational information on gratitude, including the reasons a consistent gratitude practice is so important (yet challenging) and how gratitude can affect every part of your life.

WHAT IS GRATITUDE?

Gratitude refers to a feeling of thankfulness and an expression of appreciation for who you are, what you have, and what other people have done for you, and is grounded in adopting an attitude that allows you to see the world through a lens of positivity.

When you practice gratitude, you focus on everything good in your life. Focusing on the positives means thinking about everything that is going well instead of ruminating on your fears, regrets, and problems. Saying thank you to a stranger who holds the door open for you, letting your child know how much you enjoyed their hug, and being thankful for the ability to hug your child back are all ways of expressing gratitude. This can enhance your mood and improve your emotional well-being—it's hard to focus on negative feelings when you're conscious of all your blessings.

HOW GRATITUDE AFFECTS EVERY AREA OF YOUR LIFE

Gratitude is a practice that delivers universal benefits. According to Robert A. Emmons, the world's leading expert on gratitude, there is not one area of life that doesn't improve when we use gratitude as the lens through which to view it.

After studying more than one thousand participants between the ages of eight and eighty, Emmons reports that people who regularly practice gratitude experience a wide range of benefits by maintaining the habit, including the following:

- **Psychological wellness:** When it comes to emotional well-being, people who practice gratitude consistently tend to be happier, more optimistic, and more satisfied with life than those without a consistent practice.

- **Social benefits:** When it comes to social relationships and interactions, those with a consistent gratitude practice typically feel less lonely and isolated and embrace feeling more outgoing, forgiving, compassionate, and generous. A regular gratitude practice can improve your interpersonal relationships, too. Expressing appreciation for your partner creates a more peaceful, loving environment where you focus on positive things, which makes it easier to find forgiveness, avoid arguments, and find satisfaction in your relationship.

- **Physical benefits:** People who practice gratitude every day also tend to experience improved physical health—lower blood pressure, stronger immune systems, longer and deeper sleep, and fewer aches and pains. They exercise more, too.

Additionally, gratitude and positive emotions operate in a synergistic manner: Gratitude strengthens our ability to cope with stress and encourages us to live in and celebrate the present, whereas positive emotions like happiness help us recognize who or what to be grateful for each day. The points listed earlier are just a few of the benefits people gain from practicing gratitude. So don't stop practicing after the sixty days are up—gratitude journaling is a habit you can keep for the rest of your life.

WHY IS GRATITUDE A CHALLENGE?

Gratitude counteracts our natural negativity bias, which is how the brain has evolved to help us stay alert for and aware of potential threats to our survival by focusing on what could go wrong.

However, now that we are no longer hunter-gatherers, this negativity bias can easily distort our view of what we observe, both within and around us. Even our everyday challenges, such as thoughts like *I can't get through this textbook!* or *My boss is disappointed in me,* or frustrating experiences like being stuck in traffic or dealing with a child having a temper tantrum, can activate the same physiological responses—heart pounding, blood racing, and difficulty accessing logic and reason—just as a real life-threatening experience would.

Gratitude helps us shift toward a positive viewpoint by looking for and focusing on the good, rather than being drawn to and seeing only the bad.

YOUR THOUGHTS DON'T DEFINE YOU

Negative thinking is a powerful, painful, and penetrating state of mind. It's also easier to slip into than thinking positively, and negative thoughts and experiences tend to outweigh their positive counterparts.

Let's say you're having a phenomenal day. But then someone says something that gets under your skin. Suddenly, your positive day turns sour. You're angry. You're feeling all sorts of negative emotions. Remember this: *What you focus on is what you feel.* Instead of allowing yourself to spiral into a mindset of negativity, stop and begin to name things you can feel grateful for in that moment. This helps you snap out of the negative spiral and brings you back to the present. It also changes your focus, bringing positivity back to the forefront of your brain. Continuing to focus your thoughts in this way helps you realize how much you've got to be grateful for.

Negative thinking is a habit. But here's the secret: so is positive thinking. You can choose to develop it. This doesn't mean denying reality or ignoring difficulties. But you can decide to choose positivity over negativity.

HOW A GRATITUDE JOURNAL CAN HELP

Keeping a journal is a good way to consistently practice gratitude. Regularly writing down all the things you are grateful for helps increase feelings of positivity and happiness, improves self-esteem, and makes managing stress easier.

A gratitude journal practice is a good reminder to focus on the positive because it allows you to either begin or end your day by writing down the things that bring you joy and happiness. This tool can help you become the best version of yourself. Here are just a few of its benefits:

- If you struggle with anger, gratitude journaling can help you find some calm in chaotic situations.

- If you're never satisfied, gratitude journaling can help you uncover all the things you can be genuinely thankful for.

- If you find it difficult to tap in to a sense of awareness and intention about the direction in which your life is headed, gratitude journaling can help with that, too.

TAKE SMALL STEPS TOWARD BUILDING A GRATITUDE PRACTICE EVERY DAY

Building a consistent gratitude practice doesn't require much at all—just a few minutes of your time each day. Best of all, the more you practice gratitude, the more you *want* to practice gratitude. That's because it releases the feel-good neurotransmitters serotonin and dopamine, which create positive feelings that motivate you to repeat these behaviors. A 2010 study by Adam Grant and Francesca Gino published in the *Journal of Personality and Social Psychology* found that gratitude also leads to prosocial behavior, which benefits both the individual and society. So, as you embark on this sixty-day journey of gratitude, remember that you'll not only feel the benefits of this practice now, you will also positively impact the lives of those around you, creating a better future.

Regardless of your starting point, by dedicating time every day to this gratitude practice, you can begin to shift the way you move through the world, and consequently feel happier and approach the world with a brighter outlook. The more you practice, the easier it becomes.

PART TWO

DAILY CHECK-IN

It's time to spread your wings and start journaling. Begin each day by filling out the daily tracker section. This will help you start your day with a gratitude mindset. You don't have to fill in everything but do try to challenge yourself to complete as much as you can.

Date—Fill in the date and day of the week.

Mood Tracker—Track your current mood by circling one of the emojis.

Energy Tracker—Track how much energy your body has: low, medium, or high.

Mind-Body Tracker—Identify the physical and mental symptoms you're currently experiencing.

Today I'm Grateful For—Fill in something you're grateful for today.

Daily Gratitude Goals—Write down any gratitude-related goals you have for the day.

Today's Affirmation or Intention—Identify a positive affirmation for your day. Or you may identify something you want to focus on throughout your day.

Next, turn to the day's reflective prompt, practice, or tip. These tools will help you dive deeper into your gratitude practice.

Reflective Prompts are questions or statements that encourage you to think about gratitude and document it.

Practices offer you something you can do to care for yourself and help boost your gratitude, such as meditation, a body scan, or mindful breathing.

PRACTICE

Lie down on your back in a comfortable place. Starting with your toes, tense and release your muscles by squeezing tightly as you breathe in and letting go as you breathe out. Then, move on to your feet, legs, glutes, abdomen, back, hands, arms, shoulders, and neck before ending with your face. As you do this, think of something you can be grateful for about each body part and write it below.

DAY 4

Date/Day _____

Mood Tracker 😐 ☹ 😐 😊 😄

Energy Tracker 🔋 🔋 🔋

Mind-Body Tracker

☐ Energized   ☐ Achy   ☐ Relaxed
☐ Tired   ☐ Sluggish   ☐ Well-rested
☐ Refreshed   ☐ Creative   ☐ Jittery
☐ Weak   ☐ Numb   ☐ Strong
☐ _____   ☐ _____   ☐ _____

Today I'm Grateful For . . .

_____

_____

_____

Daily Gratitude Goals

1. _____

2. _____

3. _____

Today's Affirmation or Intention:

_____

_____

_____

TIP

Think of a time or two when you had difficulty being kind or thoughtful toward others. Perhaps you had a bad day or felt slighted. The next time you find yourself in this position, step away for a moment and reflect on something good in your life—gratitude and a generous spirit may be the very things you need to help turn your mood around. Write down a few of those good things below, so you can revisit that list when you find yourself in that position again.

DAY 5

Date/Day _____

Mood Tracker 😤 😦 😐 😃 😆

Energy Tracker 🔋 🔋 🔋

Mind-Body Tracker

☐ Energized   ☐ Achy   ☐ Relaxed
☐ Tired   ☐ Sluggish   ☐ Well-rested
☐ Refreshed   ☐ Creative   ☐ Jittery
☐ Weak   ☐ Numb   ☐ Strong
☐ _____   ☐ _____   ☐ _____

Today I'm Grateful For . . .

_____

_____

_____

Daily Gratitude Goals

1. _____

2. _____

3. _____

Today's Affirmation or Intention:

_____

_____

_____

REFLECTIVE PROMPT

Think about something you have in your life now that you are grateful for, but that you wouldn't have if you hadn't endured a challenge first. Perhaps it's a qualification, a skill, a job title, or a fitness level. What was the hardest part of that challenge, and how did you overcome it?

DAY 6

Date/Day _____

Mood Tracker (ToT) ☹ 😐 🙂 😆

Energy Tracker 🔋 🔋 🔋

Mind-Body Tracker

☐ Energized ☐ Achy ☐ Relaxed
☐ Tired ☐ Sluggish ☐ Well-rested
☐ Refreshed ☐ Creative ☐ Jittery
☐ Weak ☐ Numb ☐ Strong
☐ _____ ☐ _____ ☐ _____

Today I'm Grateful For . . .

_____

_____

_____

Daily Gratitude Goals

1. _____

2. _____

3. _____

Today's Affirmation or Intention:

_____

_____

_____

REFLECTIVE PROMPT

Write about an experience that didn't seem funny at the time, but makes you laugh out loud whenever you think about it now. Why do you think you are able to laugh about it now? Why are you grateful for that memory and the laughter it brought?

_____

_____

_____

_____

_____

_____

_____

_____

_____

_____

_____

_____

_____

DAY 7

Date/Day _____

Mood Tracker 😠 🙁 😐 🙂 😆

Energy Tracker 🔋 🔋 🔋

Mind-Body Tracker

☐ Energized ☐ Achy ☐ Relaxed
☐ Tired ☐ Sluggish ☐ Well-rested
☐ Refreshed ☐ Creative ☐ Jittery
☐ Weak ☐ Numb ☐ Strong
☐ _____ ☐ _____ ☐ _____

Today I'm Grateful For . . .

_____

_____

_____

Daily Gratitude Goals

1. _____

2. _____

3. _____

Today's Affirmation or Intention:

_____

_____

_____

TIP

Today, when you are out and about, pay attention to the things that you see. Find three or more things that you never really noticed before, write them down below, and then express gratitude for them. Reflect on how focusing on these things shifts your mood and how it makes you feel. For example, do you feel more optimistic or less stressed after reflecting on something positive?

DAY 8

Date/Day _____

Mood Tracker 😭 🙁 😐 🙂 😆

Energy Tracker 🔋 🔋 🔋

Mind-Body Tracker

☐ Energized   ☐ Achy   ☐ Relaxed
☐ Tired   ☐ Sluggish   ☐ Well-rested
☐ Refreshed   ☐ Creative   ☐ Jittery
☐ Weak   ☐ Numb   ☐ Strong
☐ _____   ☐ _____   ☐ _____

Today I'm Grateful For . . .

_____

_____

_____

Daily Gratitude Goals

1. _____

2. _____

3. _____

Today's Affirmation or Intention:

_____

_____

_____

PRACTICE

This breathing practice will help you express appreciation for yourself.

1. Find a comfortable and quiet place. Take a seat. Set a timer for five minutes.

2. Close your eyes and think of all the gratitude and appreciation you've cultivated for yourself.

3. Inhale slowly and deeply to the count of five, then exhale slowly and deeply to the count of five. Repeat this pattern for the remainder of your session.

4. When you hear the timer, gently open your eyes and exit your session with an expression of gratitude.

5. Reflect on your practice below.

_____

_____

_____

_____

_____

_____

_____

_____

_____

_____

DAY 9

Date/Day _____

Mood Tracker 😭 🙁 😐 🙂 😆

Energy Tracker 🔋 🔋 🔋

Mind-Body Tracker

☐ Energized   ☐ Achy   ☐ Relaxed

☐ Tired   ☐ Sluggish   ☐ Well-rested

☐ Refreshed   ☐ Creative   ☐ Jittery

☐ Weak   ☐ Numb   ☐ Strong

☐ _____   ☐ _____   ☐ _____

Today I'm Grateful For . . .

_____

_____

_____

Daily Gratitude Goals

1. _____

2. _____

3. _____

Today's Affirmation or Intention:

_____

_____

_____

REFLECTIVE PROMPT

Think of a time in your life when you felt different from everyone else, perhaps when you moved to a new town or started a new job. How did that make you feel, and how did it help you appreciate your differences and turn them into strengths?

_____

_____

_____

_____

_____

_____

_____

_____

_____

_____

_____

_____

_____

_____

_____

_____

DAY 10

Date/Day _____

Mood Tracker 😣 🙁 😐 😃 😆

Energy Tracker 🔋 🔋 🔋

Mind-Body Tracker

☐ Energized   ☐ Achy   ☐ Relaxed
☐ Tired   ☐ Sluggish   ☐ Well-rested
☐ Refreshed   ☐ Creative   ☐ Jittery
☐ Weak   ☐ Numb   ☐ Strong
☐ _____   ☐ _____ ☐ _____

Today I'm Grateful For . . .

_____

_____

_____

Daily Gratitude Goals

1. _____

2. _____

3. _____

Today's Affirmation or Intention:

_____

_____

_____

PRACTICE

Spend some time in nature today. You can go for a hike, climb a mountain, sit by a lake, go to the beach, or simply walk in the park. Take deep breaths and notice everything you see, hear, smell, and feel. Allow the peace and tranquility of the moment to wash over you as you experience nature. Reflect on the experience below.

_____

_____

_____

_____

_____

_____

_____

_____

_____

_____

_____

_____

_____

_____

_____

DAY 11

Date/Day _____

Mood Tracker 😵 🙁 😐 😄 😆

Energy Tracker 🔋 🔋 🔋

Mind-Body Tracker

☐ Energized   ☐ Achy   ☐ Relaxed
☐ Tired   ☐ Sluggish   ☐ Well-rested
☐ Refreshed   ☐ Creative   ☐ Jittery
☐ Weak   ☐ Numb   ☐ Strong
☐ _____   ☐ _____ ☐ _____

Today I'm Grateful For . . .

_____

_____

_____

Daily Gratitude Goals

1. _____

2. _____

3. _____

Today's Affirmation or Intention:

_____

_____

_____

REFLECTIVE PROMPT

Which of your senses evokes memories most strongly? Are you most affected by the smell of something? A song? A photo of a particular place? What feelings do these things evoke, and how can you tap into those emotions as part of your gratitude practice?

_____

_____

_____

_____

_____

_____

_____

_____

_____

_____

_____

_____

_____

_____

_____

_____

_____

DAY 12

Date/Day _____

Mood Tracker 😡 ☹️ 😐 🙂 😄

Energy Tracker 🔋 🔋 🔋

Mind-Body Tracker

☐ Energized   ☐ Achy   ☐ Relaxed

☐ Tired   ☐ Sluggish   ☐ Well-rested

☐ Refreshed   ☐ Creative   ☐ Jittery

☐ Weak   ☐ Numb   ☐ Strong

☐ _____   ☐ _____   ☐ _____

Today I'm Grateful For . . .

_____

_____

_____

Daily Gratitude Goals

1. _____

2. _____

3. _____

Today's Affirmation or Intention:

_____

_____

_____

TIP

The human brain evolved to focus on the negative as a means of survival. What that translates to in today's world is this: If you are given ten compliments and one criticism, you will likely focus on the criticism.

Neuroscience has shown that we can literally rewire our brains toward being happier and healthier. This begins with an awareness of our thoughts and recognizing when our mind's attention is stuck on the negative. With compassion, work toward focusing your attention on something positive. Anytime your mind wanders back to the negative, simply invite your attention back to the bright side. Eventually, your habits will change. Jot down a few positive things below that you can focus on anytime you find yourself dwelling on the negative.

DAY 13

Date/Day _____

Mood Tracker 😡 ☹️ 😐 🙂 😆

Energy Tracker 🔋 🔋 🔋

Mind-Body Tracker

☐ Energized   ☐ Achy   ☐ Relaxed
☐ Tired   ☐ Sluggish   ☐ Well-rested
☐ Refreshed   ☐ Creative   ☐ Jittery
☐ Weak   ☐ Numb   ☐ Strong
☐ _____   ☐ _____   ☐ _____

Today I'm Grateful For . . .

_____

_____

_____

Daily Gratitude Goals

1. _____

2. _____

3. _____

Today's Affirmation or Intention:

_____

_____

_____

Think of one random act of kindness you can do today for someone you don't know. It can be a small thing, like giving up your seat on the bus, buying someone a coffee, or writing an anonymous thank-you note. Think about how you feel while planning it and how you feel when you do it, and reflect on that below. How could you make this a more regular practice in your life?

DAY 14

Date/Day _____

Mood Tracker (ToT) ☹ 😐 😀 😆

Energy Tracker 🔋 🔋 🔋

Mind-Body Tracker

☐ Energized	☐ Achy	☐ Relaxed
☐ Tired	☐ Sluggish	☐ Well-rested
☐ Refreshed	☐ Creative	☐ Jittery
☐ Weak	☐ Numb	☐ Strong
☐ _____	☐ _____	☐ _____

Today I'm Grateful For . . .

_____

_____

_____

Daily Gratitude Goals

1. _____

2. _____

3. _____

Today's Affirmation or Intention:

_____

_____

_____

REFLECTIVE PROMPT

Describe your daily routine and what you like most about it.
Why are you grateful for your daily routine?

_____

_____

_____

_____

_____

_____

_____

_____

_____

_____

_____

_____

_____

_____

_____

_____

_____

_____

DAY 15

Date/Day _____

Mood Tracker 😡 🙁 😐 🙂 😄

Energy Tracker 🔋 🔋 🔋

Mind-Body Tracker

☐ Energized	☐ Achy	☐ Relaxed
☐ Tired	☐ Sluggish	☐ Well-rested
☐ Refreshed	☐ Creative	☐ Jittery
☐ Weak	☐ Numb	☐ Strong
☐ _____	☐ _____	☐ _____

Today I'm Grateful For . . .

_____

_____

_____

Daily Gratitude Goals

1. _____

2. _____

3. _____

Today's Affirmation or Intention:

_____

_____

_____

REFLECTIVE PROMPT

Think about something you read that changed the way you look at the world. What did you learn? In what ways did it move you? Why was it so meaningful?

_____

_____

_____

_____

_____

_____

_____

_____

_____

_____

_____

_____

_____

_____

_____

_____

_____

DAY 16

Date/Day _____

Mood Tracker 🫤 ☹️ 😐 😃 😆

Energy Tracker 🔋 🔋 🔋

Mind-Body Tracker

☐ Energized   ☐ Achy   ☐ Relaxed

☐ Tired   ☐ Sluggish   ☐ Well-rested

☐ Refreshed   ☐ Creative   ☐ Jittery

☐ Weak   ☐ Numb   ☐ Strong

☐ _____   ☐ _____   ☐ _____

Today I'm Grateful For . . .

_____

_____

_____

Daily Gratitude Goals

1. _____

2. _____

3. _____

Today's Affirmation or Intention:

_____

_____

_____

PRACTICE

Write a letter to a teacher or mentor who had a strong impact on you, either in childhood or later in life. Explain how they impacted your life and what it meant to you. Why are you grateful for this person? If you can, share the letter with them.

DAY 17

Date/Day _____

Mood Tracker 😭 ☹️ 😐 🙂 😆

Energy Tracker 🔋 🔋 🔋

Mind-Body Tracker

☐ Energized   ☐ Achy   ☐ Relaxed

☐ Tired   ☐ Sluggish   ☐ Well-rested

☐ Refreshed   ☐ Creative   ☐ Jittery

☐ Weak   ☐ Numb   ☐ Strong

☐ _____   ☐ _____   ☐ _____

Today I'm Grateful For . . .

_____

_____

_____

Daily Gratitude Goals

1. _____

2. _____

3. _____

Today's Affirmation or Intention:

_____

_____

_____

PRACTICE

Today's practice will help you wind down by mindfully drinking your favorite beverage (such as coffee, tea, or wine) with awareness, gratitude, and presence.

1. Be mindful and intentional as you pour the beverage into a glass.

2. Take a deep breath in through your nose, noticing any smells; exhale out anything standing in your way of being present.

3. Slowly take a sip, mindfully tuning in to all your senses as you taste it. Notice the flavors and sensations you are experiencing.

4. Be grateful for this moment as you slow down, sip, and savor.

5. Reflect on your experience below.

DAY 18

Date/Day _____

Mood Tracker (ToT) ☹ 😐 😊 😆

Energy Tracker 🔋 🔋 🔋

Mind-Body Tracker

☐ Energized   ☐ Achy   ☐ Relaxed

☐ Tired   ☐ Sluggish   ☐ Well-rested

☐ Refreshed   ☐ Creative   ☐ Jittery

☐ Weak   ☐ Numb   ☐ Strong

☐ _____   ☐ _____   ☐ _____

Today I'm Grateful For . . .

_____

_____

_____

Daily Gratitude Goals

1. _____

2. _____

3. _____

Today's Affirmation or Intention:

_____

_____

_____

REFLECTIVE PROMPT

Reflect on your thoughts, emotions, and viewpoints as a child. In what ways do children view the world differently from adults, and how can you incorporate that perspective into your life?

_____

_____

_____

_____

_____

_____

_____

_____

_____

_____

_____

_____

_____

_____

_____

_____

DAY 19

Date/Day _____

Mood Tracker 😡 ☹️ 😐 🙂 😆

Energy Tracker 🔋 🔋 🔋

Mind-Body Tracker

☐ Energized   ☐ Achy   ☐ Relaxed

☐ Tired   ☐ Sluggish   ☐ Well-rested

☐ Refreshed   ☐ Creative   ☐ Jittery

☐ Weak   ☐ Numb   ☐ Strong

☐ _____   ☐ _____   ☐ _____

Today I'm Grateful For . . .

_____

_____

_____

Daily Gratitude Goals

1. _____

2. _____

3. _____

Today's Affirmation or Intention:

_____

_____

_____

TIP

Set aside an uninterrupted block of thirty minutes to read something that interests you. Think about what you are reading and what emotions come up as you read. What does it feel like to read something you enjoy? How could you make this a regular practice for yourself?

DAY 20

Date/Day _____

Mood Tracker   😠   🙁   😐   🙂   😆

Energy Tracker

Mind-Body Tracker

☐ Energized   ☐ Achy   ☐ Relaxed

☐ Tired   ☐ Sluggish   ☐ Well-rested

☐ Refreshed   ☐ Creative   ☐ Jittery

☐ Weak   ☐ Numb   ☐ Strong

☐ _____   ☐ _____   ☐ _____

Today I'm Grateful For . . .

_____

_____

_____

Daily Gratitude Goals

1. _____

2. _____

3. _____

Today's Affirmation or Intention:

_____

_____

_____

REFLECTIVE PROMPT

Sometimes we may take the simplest things for granted: Running water. Electricity. Food. A brain to help us think, dream, and plan for the future. What are three things you've taken for granted in the past but feel genuine gratitude for when you stop to reflect on them?

_____

_____

_____

_____

_____

_____

_____

_____

_____

_____

_____

_____

_____

_____

_____

_____

DAY 21

Date/Day _____

Mood Tracker 😤 ☹️ 😐 😃 😆

Energy Tracker 🔋 🔋 🔋

Mind-Body Tracker

☐ Energized	☐ Achy	☐ Relaxed
☐ Tired	☐ Sluggish	☐ Well-rested
☐ Refreshed	☐ Creative	☐ Jittery
☐ Weak	☐ Numb	☐ Strong
☐ _____	☐ _____	☐ _____

Today I'm Grateful For . . .

_____

_____

_____

Daily Gratitude Goals

1. _____

2. _____

3. _____

Today's Affirmation or Intention:

_____

_____

_____

PRACTICE

Designate a jar to keep notes of everything you are grateful for. On a small piece of paper, write down one thing each day or a few times a week, and place it in the jar. At the end of the month, take out all the notes and allow yourself to feel joy, recalling the moments or experiences you wrote about. Then, in the lines below, write down the three things you are most grateful for.

_____

_____

_____

_____

_____

_____

_____

_____

_____

_____

_____

_____

_____

DAY 22

Date/Day _____

Mood Tracker 😠 🙁 😐 🙂 😄

Energy Tracker 🔋 🔋 🔋

Mind-Body Tracker

☐ Energized   ☐ Achy   ☐ Relaxed
☐ Tired   ☐ Sluggish   ☐ Well-rested
☐ Refreshed   ☐ Creative   ☐ Jittery
☐ Weak   ☐ Numb   ☐ Strong
☐ _____   ☐ _____   ☐ _____

Today I'm Grateful For . . .

_____
_____
_____

Daily Gratitude Goals

1. _____

2. _____

3. _____

Today's Affirmation or Intention:

_____
_____
_____

PRACTICE

Use this breathing exercise to bring awareness to and create gratitude for your mind-body connection.

1. Lie on your back in a comfortable position.

2. Place one hand on your stomach and one hand on your chest.

3. Slowly breathe in for a count of four, sending your breath down to your stomach so that it expands and your hand rises. Your chest should remain still.

4. Tighten your abdominal muscles so your stomach contracts as you exhale for a count of seven.

5. Do this for five to ten minutes and reflect on how you feel after completing this breathing exercise.

_____

_____

_____

_____

_____

_____

_____

_____

_____

_____

DAY 23

Date/Day _____

Mood Tracker 😤 🙁 😐 🙂 😆

Energy Tracker 🔋 🔋 🔋

Mind-Body Tracker

☐ Energized   ☐ Achy   ☐ Relaxed

☐ Tired   ☐ Sluggish   ☐ Well-rested

☐ Refreshed   ☐ Creative   ☐ Jittery

☐ Weak   ☐ Numb   ☐ Strong

☐ _____   ☐ _____   ☐ _____

Today I'm Grateful For . . .

_____

_____

_____

Daily Gratitude Goals

1. _____

2. _____

3. _____

Today's Affirmation or Intention:

_____

_____

_____

REFLECTIVE PROMPT

Your self-talk determines your self-worth. Think of three empowering things you can say to yourself and write them below. Bonus points if you say them out loud to yourself today.

DAY 24

Date/Day _____

Mood Tracker   😡   ☹️   😐   😊   😆

Energy Tracker   🔋   🔋   🔋

Mind-Body Tracker

☐ Energized   ☐ Achy   ☐ Relaxed

☐ Tired   ☐ Sluggish   ☐ Well-rested

☐ Refreshed   ☐ Creative   ☐ Jittery

☐ Weak   ☐ Numb   ☐ Strong

☐ _____   ☐ _____   ☐ _____

Today I'm Grateful For . . .

_____

_____

_____

Daily Gratitude Goals

1. _____

2. _____

3. _____

Today's Affirmation or Intention:

_____

_____

_____

REFLECTIVE PROMPT

Think about the aspects of nature that calm you, energize you, bring you peace, or make you happy. What are you most grateful for in nature, and why?

_____

_____

_____

_____

_____

_____

_____

_____

_____

_____

_____

_____

_____

_____

_____

_____

DAY 25

Date/Day _____

Mood Tracker 🙃 😦 😐 😃 😆

Energy Tracker 🔋 🔋 🔋

Mind-Body Tracker

☐ Energized   ☐ Achy   ☐ Relaxed
☐ Tired   ☐ Sluggish   ☐ Well-rested
☐ Refreshed   ☐ Creative   ☐ Jittery
☐ Weak   ☐ Numb   ☐ Strong
☐ _____   ☐ _____   ☐ _____

Today I'm Grateful For . . .

_____

_____

_____

Daily Gratitude Goals

1. _____

2. _____

3. _____

Today's Affirmation or Intention:

_____

_____

_____

TIP

It's biologically impossible to feel stressed and grateful simultaneously. Think of three things to feel grateful for so that today, if you feel stress, you can stop and think of them. Write them below.

DAY 26

Date/Day _____

Mood Tracker 😫 ☹️ 😐 😃 😆

Energy Tracker 🔋 🔋 🔋

Mind-Body Tracker

☐ Energized   ☐ Achy   ☐ Relaxed
☐ Tired   ☐ Sluggish   ☐ Well-rested
☐ Refreshed   ☐ Creative   ☐ Jittery
☐ Weak   ☐ Numb   ☐ Strong
☐ _____   ☐ _____   ☐ _____

Today I'm Grateful For . . .

_____

_____

_____

Daily Gratitude Goals

1. _____

2. _____

3. _____

Today's Affirmation or Intention:

_____

_____

_____

REFLECTIVE PROMPT

How great does it feel to be you? Write down three positive qualities about yourself below. After you've written them down, take a moment to reflect on how it makes you feel to think about your own positive attributes. Sit with those feelings.

DAY 27

Date/Day _____

Mood Tracker 😖 🙁 😐 🙂 😄

Energy Tracker 🔋 🔋 🔋

Mind-Body Tracker

☐ Energized   ☐ Achy   ☐ Relaxed

☐ Tired   ☐ Sluggish   ☐ Well-rested

☐ Refreshed   ☐ Creative   ☐ Jittery

☐ Weak   ☐ Numb   ☐ Strong

☐ _____   ☐ _____   ☐ _____

Today I'm Grateful For . . .

_____

_____

_____

Daily Gratitude Goals

1. _____

2. _____

3. _____

Today's Affirmation or Intention:

_____

_____

_____

REFLECTIVE PROMPT

Recall a time when someone expressed their gratitude to you. How did that feel? Write about it below.

_____

_____

_____

_____

_____

_____

_____

_____

_____

_____

_____

_____

_____

_____

_____

_____

_____

_____

_____

DAY 28

Date/Day _____

Mood Tracker 😠 😦 😐 😃 😆

Energy Tracker 🔋 🔋 🔋

Mind-Body Tracker

☐ Energized ☐ Achy ☐ Relaxed
☐ Tired ☐ Sluggish ☐ Well-rested
☐ Refreshed ☐ Creative ☐ Jittery
☐ Weak ☐ Numb ☐ Strong
☐ _____ ☐ _____ ☐ _____

Today I'm Grateful For . . .

_____

_____

_____

Daily Gratitude Goals

1. _____

2. _____

3. _____

Today's Affirmation or Intention:

_____

_____

_____

PRACTICE

Today, meditate for one minute and focus on this moment.

1. Sit in a comfortable position, set a one-minute timer, and focus on breathing in through your nose and out through your mouth.

2. When your mind wanders, simply notice your thoughts without judgment. Bring your attention back to your breath and the sensation of inhaling and exhaling.

3. Reflect on your experience below.

_____

_____

_____

_____

_____

_____

_____

_____

_____

_____

_____

_____

_____

DAY 29

Date/Day _____

Mood Tracker 😡 ☹️ 😐 😊 😆

Energy Tracker 🔋 🔋 🔋

Mind-Body Tracker

☐ Energized   ☐ Achy   ☐ Relaxed
☐ Tired   ☐ Sluggish   ☐ Well-rested
☐ Refreshed   ☐ Creative   ☐ Jittery
☐ Weak   ☐ Numb   ☐ Strong
☐ _____   ☐ _____   ☐ _____

Today I'm Grateful For . . .

_____

_____

_____

Daily Gratitude Goals

1. _____

2. _____

3. _____

Today's Affirmation or Intention:

_____

_____

_____

TIP

Think of a time when things worked out in your favor. Maybe you had exact change to pay for what you were buying, caught the train just before the doors closed, or got a friend to pick up your kid when you were running late. Write down a few of these times below and remember that things often do go right. Revel in gratitude for the moments that went your way.

DAY 30

Date/Day _____

Mood Tracker 😑 ☹️ 😐 😃 😆

Energy Tracker 🔋 🔋 🔋

Mind-Body Tracker

☐ Energized	☐ Achy	☐ Relaxed
☐ Tired	☐ Sluggish	☐ Well-rested
☐ Refreshed	☐ Creative	☐ Jittery
☐ Weak	☐ Numb	☐ Strong
☐ _____	☐ _____	☐ _____

Today I'm Grateful For . . .

_____

_____

_____

Daily Gratitude Goals

1. _____

2. _____

3. _____

Today's Affirmation or Intention:

_____

_____

_____

REFLECTIVE PROMPT

What inspires you to get up every morning? Why?

_____

_____

_____

_____

_____

_____

_____

_____

_____

_____

_____

_____

_____

_____

_____

_____

DAY 31

Date/Day _____

Mood Tracker 😫 🙁 😐 🙂 😄

Energy Tracker 🔋 🔋 🔋

Mind-Body Tracker

☐ Energized ☐ Achy ☐ Relaxed

☐ Tired ☐ Sluggish ☐ Well-rested

☐ Refreshed ☐ Creative ☐ Jittery

☐ Weak ☐ Numb ☐ Strong

☐ _____ ☐ _____ ☐ _____

Today I'm Grateful For . . .

_____

_____

_____

Daily Gratitude Goals

1. _____

2. _____

3. _____

Today's Affirmation or Intention:

_____

_____

_____

TIP

Positive thinking isn't a magic cure for all your problems, but it's a good start. Remember, positive thinking leads to positive action, which can lead to positive outcomes. Try to choose one of your negative thought patterns each week and counteract it with a positive statement about the situation. What's one negative thought pattern you need to let go of right now? Write it below.

DAY 32

Date/Day _____

Mood Tracker 😭 ☹ 😐 🙂 😆

Energy Tracker 🔋 🔋 🔋

Mind-Body Tracker

☐ Energized   ☐ Achy   ☐ Relaxed
☐ Tired   ☐ Sluggish   ☐ Well-rested
☐ Refreshed   ☐ Creative   ☐ Jittery
☐ Weak   ☐ Numb   ☐ Strong
☐ _____   ☐ _____   ☐ _____

Today I'm Grateful For . . .

_____

_____

_____

_____

Daily Gratitude Goals

1. _____

2. _____

3. _____

Today's Affirmation or Intention:

_____

_____

_____

REFLECTIVE PROMPT

Think about the last time you challenged yourself mentally. What did you do? How did it make you feel? What makes you grateful about challenging yourself in this way?

DAY 33

Date/Day _____

Mood Tracker 😡 🙁 😐 🙂 😄

Energy Tracker 🔋 🔋 🔋

Mind-Body Tracker

☐ Energized   ☐ Achy   ☐ Relaxed
☐ Tired   ☐ Sluggish   ☐ Well-rested
☐ Refreshed   ☐ Creative   ☐ Jittery
☐ Weak   ☐ Numb   ☐ Strong
☐ _____   ☐ _____   ☐ _____

Today I'm Grateful For . . .

_____

_____

_____

Daily Gratitude Goals

1. _____

2. _____

3. _____

Today's Affirmation or Intention:

_____

_____

_____

REFLECTIVE PROMPT

Think of someone who cares about you (partner, friend, parent, child, etc.). If this person were asked to write down three specific reasons why they are grateful for you, what do you think they'd write?

DAY 34

Date/Day _____

Mood Tracker   😠   🙁   😐   🙂   😄

Energy Tracker   🔋   🔋   🔋

Mind-Body Tracker

☐ Energized   ☐ Achy   ☐ Relaxed

☐ Tired   ☐ Sluggish   ☐ Well-rested

☐ Refreshed   ☐ Creative   ☐ Jittery

☐ Weak   ☐ Numb   ☐ Strong

☐ _____   ☐ _____   ☐ _____

Today I'm Grateful For . . .

_____

_____

_____

Daily Gratitude Goals

1. _____

2. _____

3. _____

Today's Affirmation or Intention:

_____

_____

_____

PRACTICE

This breathwork practice will help you let go of current distractions and keep you from ruminating about past problems or future stresses by bringing your awareness to the present moment.

1. Find a quiet place. Take a seat. Set a timer for three minutes.

2. Close your eyes.

3. Breathe in fully through your nose and out through your mouth. Focus on your breath going in and out, and notice how it feels to fill your lungs. Repeat this pattern until your timer goes off.

4. When you hear the timer, gently open your eyes and exit with gratitude.

5. Reflect on the experience below.

_____

_____

_____

_____

_____

_____

_____

_____

DAY 35

Date/Day _____

Mood Tracker 😭 😟 😐 😃 😆

Energy Tracker 🔋 🔋 🔋

Mind-Body Tracker

☐ Energized   ☐ Achy   ☐ Relaxed

☐ Tired   ☐ Sluggish   ☐ Well-rested

☐ Refreshed   ☐ Creative   ☐ Jittery

☐ Weak   ☐ Numb   ☐ Strong

☐ _____   ☐ _____   ☐ _____

Today I'm Grateful For . . .

_____

_____

_____

Daily Gratitude Goals

1. _____

2. _____

3. _____

Today's Affirmation or Intention:

_____

_____

_____

REFLECTIVE PROMPT

Appreciating your accomplishments is a crucial component of a healthy mindset. Think of one thing you accomplished or will accomplish or one goal you achieved or will achieve today—even if it's something small. What will you do to celebrate and appreciate yourself?

_____

_____

_____

_____

_____

_____

_____

_____

_____

_____

_____

_____

_____

_____

_____

_____

DAY 36

Date/Day _____

Mood Tracker 😡 🙁 😐 😃 😆

Energy Tracker 🔋 🔋 🔋

Mind-Body Tracker

- [ ] Energized
- [ ] Tired
- [ ] Refreshed
- [ ] Weak
- [ ] _____

- [ ] Achy
- [ ] Sluggish
- [ ] Creative
- [ ] Numb
- [ ] _____

- [ ] Relaxed
- [ ] Well-rested
- [ ] Jittery
- [ ] Strong
- [ ] _____

Today I'm Grateful For . . .

_____

_____

_____

Daily Gratitude Goals

1. _____

2. _____

3. _____

Today's Affirmation or Intention:

_____

_____

_____

REFLECTIVE PROMPT

Look around you. What are three things in your immediate environment that you're grateful to have or use?

_____

_____

_____

_____

_____

_____

_____

_____

_____

_____

_____

_____

_____

_____

_____

_____

_____

DAY 37

Date/Day _____

Mood Tracker 😡 🙁 😐 😃 😆

Energy Tracker 🔋 🔋 🔋

Mind-Body Tracker

☐ Energized   ☐ Achy   ☐ Relaxed

☐ Tired   ☐ Sluggish   ☐ Well-rested

☐ Refreshed   ☐ Creative   ☐ Jittery

☐ Weak   ☐ Numb   ☐ Strong

☐ _____   ☐ _____   ☐ _____

Today I'm Grateful For . . .

_____

_____

_____

Daily Gratitude Goals

1. _____

2. _____

3. _____

Today's Affirmation or Intention:

_____

_____

_____

Give yourself some grace today. When negative self-talk starts to creep in, counter it by recalling things you like about yourself or something positive you've done. Write a few of those things below and repeat throughout the day as needed.

_____

_____

_____

_____

_____

_____

_____

_____

_____

_____

_____

_____

_____

_____

_____

_____

_____

DAY 38

Date/Day _____

Mood Tracker 😭 🙁 😐 🙂 😆

Energy Tracker 🔋 🔋 🔋

Mind-Body Tracker

☐ Energized   ☐ Achy   ☐ Relaxed

☐ Tired   ☐ Sluggish   ☐ Well-rested

☐ Refreshed   ☐ Creative   ☐ Jittery

☐ Weak   ☐ Numb   ☐ Strong

☐ _____   ☐ _____   ☐ _____

Today I'm Grateful For . . .

_____

_____

_____

Daily Gratitude Goals

1. _____

2. _____

3. _____

Today's Affirmation or Intention:

_____

_____

_____

REFLECTIVE PROMPT

What's a goal you're working on right now that, though challenging, brings you joy and happiness while you work on it?

_____

_____

_____

_____

_____

_____

_____

_____

_____

_____

_____

_____

_____

_____

_____

_____

_____

_____

DAY 39

Date/Day _____

Mood Tracker 😭 🙁 😐 🙂 😆

Energy Tracker 🔋 🔋 🔋

Mind-Body Tracker

☐ Energized   ☐ Achy   ☐ Relaxed
☐ Tired   ☐ Sluggish   ☐ Well-rested
☐ Refreshed   ☐ Creative   ☐ Jittery
☐ Weak   ☐ Numb   ☐ Strong
☐ _____   ☐ _____   ☐ _____

Today I'm Grateful For . . .

_____

_____

_____

Daily Gratitude Goals

1. _____

2. _____

3. _____

Today's Affirmation or Intention:

_____

_____

_____

REFLECTIVE PROMPT

Mini-habits are small actions you can take, practically any-time, that can have a compounding impact on your life over time. What are three positive mini-habits you've developed (or want to develop) to cultivate a sustained sense of grate-fulness in your daily life?

DAY 40

Date/Day _____

Mood Tracker 😭 🙁 😐 🙂 😆

Energy Tracker 🔋 🔋 🔋

Mind-Body Tracker

☐ Energized   ☐ Achy   ☐ Relaxed

☐ Tired   ☐ Sluggish   ☐ Well-rested

☐ Refreshed   ☐ Creative   ☐ Jittery

☐ Weak   ☐ Numb   ☐ Strong

☐ _____   ☐ _____   ☐ _____

Today I'm Grateful For . . .

_____

_____

_____

Daily Gratitude Goals

1. _____

2. _____

3. _____

Today's Affirmation or Intention:

_____

_____

_____

PRACTICE

This breathwork practice will help you energize and revitalize yourself as you start the day. Please note: This practice should only be done in the morning as you will be breathing at a slightly rapid rate.

1. Find a comfortable and quiet place. Take a seat. Set a timer for five minutes.

2. Close your eyes.

3. Begin by breathing in through your nose four times rapidly, immediately followed by breathing out through your mouth four times rapidly. Repeat this pattern until your timer goes off.

4. When you hear the timer, gently open your eyes and welcome the day with gratitude.

5. Reflect on your practice below.

_____

_____

_____

_____

_____

_____

_____

DAY 41

Date/Day _____

Mood Tracker   😭   🙁   😐   🙂   😆

Energy Tracker   🔋 🔋 🔋

Mind-Body Tracker

☐ Energized   ☐ Achy   ☐ Relaxed

☐ Tired   ☐ Sluggish   ☐ Well-rested

☐ Refreshed   ☐ Creative   ☐ Jittery

☐ Weak   ☐ Numb   ☐ Strong

☐ _____   ☐ _____   ☐ _____

Today I'm Grateful For . . .

_____

_____

_____

_____

Daily Gratitude Goals

1. _____

2. _____

3. _____

Today's Affirmation or Intention:

_____

_____

_____

_____

REFLECTIVE PROMPT

Write about a challenging time in your life when someone was there for you. What about their presence was so special? Why were you moved by their support? If you haven't already, consider sharing with them how meaningful it was for you to have their presence and support during this difficult period.

_____

_____

_____

_____

_____

_____

_____

_____

_____

_____

_____

_____

_____

_____

_____

DAY 42

Date/Day _____

Mood Tracker 😡 🙁 😐 🙂 😄

Energy Tracker 🔋 🔋 🔋

Mind-Body Tracker

☐ Energized   ☐ Achy   ☐ Relaxed

☐ Tired   ☐ Sluggish   ☐ Well-rested

☐ Refreshed   ☐ Creative   ☐ Jittery

☐ Weak   ☐ Numb   ☐ Strong

☐ _____   ☐ _____   ☐ _____

Today I'm Grateful For . . .

_____

_____

_____

Daily Gratitude Goals

1. _____

2. _____

3. _____

Today's Affirmation or Intention:

_____

_____

_____

REFLECTIVE PROMPT

Research shows that one of the ways gratitude makes an impact is the surprise factor; that is, gratitude is heightened when we are surprised by a positive outcome. Has your gratitude surprised you today? If so, how is it reflective of something you may not have expected?

_____

_____

_____

_____

_____

_____

_____

_____

_____

_____

_____

_____

_____

_____

DAY 43

Date/Day _____

Mood Tracker 😝 😦 😐 😃 😄

Energy Tracker 🔋 🔋 🔋

Mind-Body Tracker

☐ Energized   ☐ Achy   ☐ Relaxed

☐ Tired   ☐ Sluggish   ☐ Well-rested

☐ Refreshed   ☐ Creative   ☐ Jittery

☐ Weak   ☐ Numb   ☐ Strong

☐ _____   ☐ _____   ☐ _____

Today I'm Grateful For . . .

_____

_____

_____

Daily Gratitude Goals

1. _____

2. _____

3. _____

Today's Affirmation or Intention:

_____

_____

_____

TIP

When you find yourself stuck in a cycle of negative thoughts, use these three steps to regain perspective and reclaim gratitude.

1. Take a deep breath to bring yourself into the present moment.

2. Ask yourself, "What can I feel grateful about right now?" to shift your focus to positive thoughts and emotions. Write these things down.

3. Remind yourself of all the positive experiences you had throughout your day and write these down as well to help shift your perspective.

_____

_____

_____

_____

_____

_____

_____

_____

_____

_____

_____

DAY 44

Date/Day _____

Mood Tracker 😭 ☹️ 😐 🙂 😆

Energy Tracker 🔋 🔋 🔋

Mind-Body Tracker

☐ Energized   ☐ Achy   ☐ Relaxed
☐ Tired   ☐ Sluggish   ☐ Well-rested
☐ Refreshed   ☐ Creative   ☐ Jittery
☐ Weak   ☐ Numb   ☐ Strong
☐ _____   ☐ _____   ☐ _____

Today I'm Grateful For . . .

_____

_____

_____

Daily Gratitude Goals

1. _____

2. _____

3. _____

Today's Affirmation or Intention:

_____

_____

_____

REFLECTIVE PROMPT

Pause and reflect on what being a good friend means to you. Think about all the qualities and strengths that make you a great friend. Consider the ways in which your friends are lucky to have you in their lives and the ways you're lucky to have them in your life.

_____

_____

_____

_____

_____

_____

_____

_____

_____

_____

_____

_____

_____

_____

_____

DAY 45

Date/Day _____

Mood Tracker 😭 ☹️ 😐 🙂 😆

Energy Tracker 🔋 🔋 🔋

Mind-Body Tracker

☐ Energized   ☐ Achy   ☐ Relaxed
☐ Tired   ☐ Sluggish   ☐ Well-rested
☐ Refreshed   ☐ Creative   ☐ Jittery
☐ Weak   ☐ Numb   ☐ Strong
☐ _____   ☐ _____   ☐ _____

Today I'm Grateful For . . .

_____

_____

_____

Daily Gratitude Goals

1. _____

2. _____

3. _____

Today's Affirmation or Intention:

_____

_____

_____

REFLECTIVE PROMPT

Reflect on a time when you were honored or appreciated by others. What was the situation, and how did it make you feel? Recalling a past experience of receiving gratitude can help you continue to build gratitude in the present moment and carry that gratifying feeling with you into the future.

DAY 46

Date/Day _____

Mood Tracker 😡 🙁 😐 🙂 😄

Energy Tracker 🔋 🔋 🔋

Mind-Body Tracker

☐ Energized   ☐ Achy   ☐ Relaxed
☐ Tired   ☐ Sluggish   ☐ Well-rested
☐ Refreshed   ☐ Creative   ☐ Jittery
☐ Weak   ☐ Numb   ☐ Strong
☐ _____   ☐ _____   ☐ _____

Today I'm Grateful For . . .

_____

_____

_____

Daily Gratitude Goals

1. _____

2. _____

3. _____

Today's Affirmation or Intention:

_____

_____

_____

PRACTICE

Sit in a quiet place and connect with your breath. As you take a few mindful breaths to focus on the present moment, bring to your mind's attention an experience that impacted you in a significant and positive way. Reflect below on why this experience was a pivotal moment in your life. What gifts do you continue to receive from that moment?

DAY 47

Date/Day _____

Mood Tracker 😭 ☹ 😐 🙂 😆

Energy Tracker 🔋 🔋 🔋

Mind-Body Tracker

☐ Energized ☐ Achy ☐ Relaxed
☐ Tired ☐ Sluggish ☐ Well-rested
☐ Refreshed ☐ Creative ☐ Jittery
☐ Weak ☐ Numb ☐ Strong
☐ _____ ☐ _____ ☐ _____

Today I'm Grateful For . . .

_____

_____

_____

Daily Gratitude Goals

1. _____

2. _____

3. _____

Today's Affirmation or Intention:

_____

_____

_____

REFLECTIVE PROMPT

What is one scent that makes you nostalgic whenever you smell it and why? What about it is meaningful to you?

_____

_____

_____

_____

_____

_____

_____

_____

_____

_____

_____

_____

_____

_____

_____

_____

_____

_____

DAY 48

Date/Day _____

Mood Tracker 😤 ☹️ 😐 🙂 😄

Energy Tracker 🔋 🔋 🔋

Mind-Body Tracker

☐ Energized   ☐ Achy   ☐ Relaxed
☐ Tired   ☐ Sluggish   ☐ Well-rested
☐ Refreshed   ☐ Creative   ☐ Jittery
☐ Weak   ☐ Numb   ☐ Strong
☐ _____   ☐ _____   ☐ _____

Today I'm Grateful For . . .

_____

_____

_____

Daily Gratitude Goals

1. _____

2. _____

3. _____

Today's Affirmation or Intention:

_____

_____

_____

TIP

Remember, you can draw upon positive memories anytime you need a boost in mood, energy, or mindset. Reflect below on one of your favorite experiences of the previous year. Be specific as you recall the details and enlist all your senses to embody this memory. Notice how it feels in your body to remember a time that brought you such happiness. In moments when you need a lift, use this mindfulness exercise to bring you back to the present and focus on the positive.

DAY 49

Date/Day _____

Mood Tracker 😤 🙁 😐 🙂 😄

Energy Tracker 🔋 🔋 🔋

Mind-Body Tracker

☐ Energized ☐ Achy ☐ Relaxed
☐ Tired ☐ Sluggish ☐ Well-rested
☐ Refreshed ☐ Creative ☐ Jittery
☐ Weak ☐ Numb ☐ Strong
☐ _____ ☐ _____ ☐ _____

Today I'm Grateful For . . .

_____

_____

_____

Daily Gratitude Goals

1. _____

2. _____

3. _____

Today's Affirmation or Intention:

_____

_____

_____

REFLECTIVE PROMPT

Think about a time when you had a positive experience in nature that stayed with you, whether it was a relaxing day at the beach, a fun picnic in a park, or an energizing walk in the woods. What stands out to you the most about that day?

DAY 50

Date/Day _____

Mood Tracker 😡 😦 😐 😃 😆

Energy Tracker 🔋 🔋 🔋

Mind-Body Tracker

☐ Energized	☐ Achy	☐ Relaxed
☐ Tired	☐ Sluggish	☐ Well-rested
☐ Refreshed	☐ Creative	☐ Jittery
☐ Weak	☐ Numb	☐ Strong
☐ _____	☐ _____	☐ _____

Today I'm Grateful For . . .

_____

_____

_____

Daily Gratitude Goals

1. _____

2. _____

3. _____

Today's Affirmation or Intention:

_____

_____

_____

PRACTICE

Take a few moments to dwell in joy today with this practice.

1. Find a comfortable place to sit. Set a timer for five minutes.

2. Visualize something that brings you joy.

3. Breathe it in, allowing joy to fill you up from your core to your heart to your mind's eye. Exhale out anything standing in the way of you embodying this joy.

4. If you get distracted, come back to your joyful visualization through your breath.

5. Reflect on your experience below.

DAY 51

Date/Day _____

Mood Tracker 😡 🙁 😐 🙂 😄

Energy Tracker 🔋 🔋 🔋

Mind-Body Tracker

☐ Energized	☐ Achy	☐ Relaxed
☐ Tired	☐ Sluggish	☐ Well-rested
☐ Refreshed	☐ Creative	☐ Jittery
☐ Weak	☐ Numb	☐ Strong
☐ _____	☐ _____	☐ _____

Today I'm Grateful For . . .

_____

_____

_____

Daily Gratitude Goals

1. _____

2. _____

3. _____

Today's Affirmation or Intention:

_____

_____

_____

PRACTICE

Think about a time when you were hurt or experienced pain or sadness. Write a gentle letter to yourself below, reflecting on that moment from a perspective of love, caring, and comfort, telling yourself all the things you wish you had heard in that painful moment. Revisit this exercise whenever you need to as a way of healing the wounds from your past.

DAY 52

Date/Day _____

Mood Tracker 🙁 😟 😐 😃 😄

Energy Tracker 🔋 🔋 🔋

Mind-Body Tracker

☐ Energized ☐ Achy ☐ Relaxed
☐ Tired ☐ Sluggish ☐ Well-rested
☐ Refreshed ☐ Creative ☐ Jittery
☐ Weak ☐ Numb ☐ Strong
☐ _____ ☐ _____ ☐ _____

Today I'm Grateful For . . .

_____

_____

_____

Daily Gratitude Goals

1. _____

2. _____

3. _____

Today's Affirmation or Intention:

_____

_____

_____

TIP

When you're feeling discouraged because of a challenge or difficulty, consider how you can reframe your thoughts about how you are relating to it. Rather than dwelling on the hard parts, reflect on how you will grow positively from the challenge. Be proud of the strengths and resources you are drawing on to get yourself through it, and remind yourself of what you've overcome in the past below.

_____

_____

_____

_____

_____

_____

_____

_____

_____

_____

_____

_____

_____

_____

DAY 53

Date/Day _____

Mood Tracker 😡 ☹️ 😐 😃 😆

Energy Tracker 🔋 🔋 🔋

Mind-Body Tracker

☐ Energized   ☐ Achy   ☐ Relaxed
☐ Tired   ☐ Sluggish   ☐ Well-rested
☐ Refreshed   ☐ Creative   ☐ Jittery
☐ Weak   ☐ Numb   ☐ Strong
☐ _____   ☐ _____   ☐ _____

Today I'm Grateful For . . .

_____

_____

_____

Daily Gratitude Goals

1. _____

2. _____

3. _____

Today's Affirmation or Intention:

_____

_____

_____

Morning rituals are a wonderful way to start your day grounded and rooted in gratitude. When you do your morning tasks today, such as watering your plants, emptying the dishwasher, or making your bed, notice the energy that you are bringing to the chore. If you are feeling negative about what you have to do, reframe it as what you *get* to do. Reflect on your morning task gratitude practice below.

DAY 54

Date/Day _____

Mood Tracker 😫 🙁 😐 😃 😆

Energy Tracker 🔋 🔋 🔋

Mind-Body Tracker

☐ Energized   ☐ Achy   ☐ Relaxed
☐ Tired   ☐ Sluggish   ☐ Well-rested
☐ Refreshed   ☐ Creative   ☐ Jittery
☐ Weak   ☐ Numb   ☐ Strong
☐ _____   ☐ _____   ☐ _____

Today I'm Grateful For . . .

_____

_____

_____

Daily Gratitude Goals

1. _____

2. _____

3. _____

Today's Affirmation or Intention:

_____

_____

_____

REFLECTIVE PROMPT

Bring to mind the most memorable trip you've ever taken. Describe it below and reflect on why it was so meaningful.

_____

_____

_____

_____

_____

_____

_____

_____

_____

_____

_____

_____

_____

_____

_____

_____

_____

_____

_____

DAY 55

Date/Day _____

Mood Tracker 😠 🙁 😐 😃 😆

Energy Tracker 🔋 🔋 🔋

Mind-Body Tracker

☐ Energized   ☐ Achy   ☐ Relaxed
☐ Tired   ☐ Sluggish   ☐ Well-rested
☐ Refreshed   ☐ Creative   ☐ Jittery
☐ Weak   ☐ Numb   ☐ Strong
☐ _____   ☐ _____   ☐ _____

Today I'm Grateful For . . .

_____

_____

_____

Daily Gratitude Goals

1. _____

2. _____

3. _____

Today's Affirmation or Intention:

_____

_____

_____

PRACTICE

Find an empty wall space, bulletin board, or scrapbook, or use the space below, and fill it with gratitude. Anytime you feel inspired by something you are grateful for, grab a sticky note or a small piece of paper, write down your source of gratitude, and add it to your collection—or bookmark this page and jot it down. Watch your gratitude collection grow and relish all the goodness in your life.

DAY 56

Date/Day _____

Mood Tracker 😭 🙁 😐 😃 😆

Energy Tracker 🔋 🔋 🔋

Mind-Body Tracker

☐ Energized	☐ Achy	☐ Relaxed
☐ Tired	☐ Sluggish	☐ Well-rested
☐ Refreshed	☐ Creative	☐ Jittery
☐ Weak	☐ Numb	☐ Strong
☐ _____	☐ _____	☐ _____

Today I'm Grateful For . . .

_____

_____

_____

Daily Gratitude Goals

1. _____

2. _____

3. _____

Today's Affirmation or Intention:

_____

_____

_____

PRACTICE

Take a mindful moment today.

1. Pause, breathe, and visualize something positive in your mind, imprinting it in your memory.

2. Take a mental snapshot of what's arising, without labeling it, and notice how it feels.

3. Close your eyes again and take a deep breath in, holding the moment in your heart.

4. Reflect on that moment below.

_____

_____

_____

_____

_____

_____

_____

_____

_____

_____

_____

_____

DAY 57

Date/Day _____

Mood Tracker (ToT) ☹ 😐 😃 😁

Energy Tracker 🔋 🔋 🔋

Mind-Body Tracker

☐ Energized ☐ Achy ☐ Relaxed
☐ Tired ☐ Sluggish ☐ Well-rested
☐ Refreshed ☐ Creative ☐ Jittery
☐ Weak ☐ Numb ☐ Strong
☐ _____ ☐ _____ ☐ _____

Today I'm Grateful For . . .

_____

_____

_____

Daily Gratitude Goals

1. _____

2. _____

3. _____

Today's Affirmation or Intention:

_____

_____

_____

TIP

Think of three things you appreciate about someone you love (a partner, a friend, or a family member—anything goes), write those things below, and then tell them if possible. Make it a habit (or even a fun daily ritual) to express your gratitude and appreciation for even the smallest of things. Every relationship can benefit from a positivity boost.

DAY 58

Date/Day _____

Mood Tracker 😡 🙁 😐 🙂 😆

Energy Tracker 🔋 🔋 🔋

Mind-Body Tracker

☐ Energized   ☐ Achy   ☐ Relaxed
☐ Tired   ☐ Sluggish   ☐ Well-rested
☐ Refreshed   ☐ Creative   ☐ Jittery
☐ Weak   ☐ Numb   ☐ Strong
☐ _____   ☐ _____   ☐ _____

Today I'm Grateful For . . .

_____

_____

_____

Daily Gratitude Goals

1. _____

2. _____

3. _____

Today's Affirmation or Intention:

_____

_____

_____

REFLECTIVE PROMPT

Teaching is the greatest form of learning. Who can you inspire today with what you've learned about yourself and the power of gratitude?

_____

_____

_____

_____

_____

_____

_____

_____

_____

_____

_____

_____

_____

_____

_____

DAY 59

Date/Day _____

Mood Tracker 😫 😟 😐 😊 😄

Energy Tracker 🔋 🔋 🔋

Mind-Body Tracker

☐ Energized	☐ Achy	☐ Relaxed
☐ Tired	☐ Sluggish	☐ Well-rested
☐ Refreshed	☐ Creative	☐ Jittery
☐ Weak	☐ Numb	☐ Strong
☐ _____	☐ _____	☐ _____

Today I'm Grateful For . . .

_____

_____

_____

Daily Gratitude Goals

1. _____

2. _____

3. _____

Today's Affirmation or Intention:

_____

_____

_____

REFLECTIVE PROMPT

After nearly sixty days of practice, what does gratitude mean to you now?

_____

_____

_____

_____

_____

_____

_____

_____

_____

_____

_____

_____

_____

_____

_____

_____

_____

_____

_____

DAY 60

Date/Day _____

Mood Tracker 😭 ☹️ 😐 🙂 😆

Energy Tracker 🔋 🔋 🔋

Mind-Body Tracker

☐ Energized   ☐ Achy   ☐ Relaxed
☐ Tired   ☐ Sluggish   ☐ Well-rested
☐ Refreshed   ☐ Creative   ☐ Jittery
☐ Weak   ☐ Numb   ☐ Strong
☐ _____   ☐ _____   ☐ _____

Today I'm Grateful For . . .

_____

_____

_____

Daily Gratitude Goals

1. _____

2. _____

3. _____

Today's Affirmation or Intention:

_____

_____

_____

TIP

It's often easier to stay committed to a new habit when we have someone to walk the new path with us. To continue your daily gratitude practice, name a friend below who might be willing to be your accountability partner, and ask them to join you. How can you support and inspire each other on your gratitude journey?

RESOURCES

BOOKS

Buddha's Brain by Rick Hanson

Gratitude Works! by Robert A. Emmons

Hardwiring Happiness by Rick Hanson

Just One Thing by Rick Hanson

The Little Book of Gratitude by Robert A. Emmons

The Psychology of Gratitude, edited by Robert A. Emmons and Michael E. McCullough

A Simple Act of Gratitude by John Kralik

Thanks! by Robert A. Emmons

Wherever You Go, There You Are by Jon Kabat-Zinn

MOBILE APPS

365 Gratitude Journal for iOS and Android

PODCASTS

The Gratitude Podcast by Georgian Benta, GeorgianBenta.com

The Positive Psychology Podcast by Kristen Truempy, play.acast
.com/s/thepositivepsychologypodcastbringingthescienceof
happinesstoyourearbudswithkristentruempy

WEBSITES

A Network for Grateful Living, Gratefulness.org

Positive Psychology, PositivePsychology.com

Thnx4, University of California, Berkeley's Greater Good Science
Center, Thnx4.org

REFERENCES

Emmons, Robert. "Why Gratitude Is Good." *Greater Good Magazine*. Greater Good Science Center, November 16, 2010. greatergood.berkeley.edu/article/item/why_gratitude_is _good.

Ferriss, Tim. *Tools of Titans: The Tactics, Routines, and Habits of Billionaires, Icons, and World-Class Performers*. Boston: Houghton Mifflin Harcourt, 2017.

Grant, Adam M., and Francesca Gino. "A Little Thanks Goes a Long Way: Explaining Why Gratitude Expressions Motivate Prosocial Behavior." *Journal of Personality and Social Psychology* 98, no. 6 (June 2010): 946–955. doi.org/10.1037 /a0017935.

"Gratitude Is Good Medicine." UC Davis Health, November 25, 2015. health.ucdavis.edu/medicalcenter/features /2015-2016/11/20151125_gratitude.html.

Haidt, Jonathan. *The Happiness Hypothesis: Putting Ancient Wisdom to the Test of Modern Science*. London: Cornerstone Digital, 2015.

Lyubomirsky, Sonja. "Expressing Gratitude." Gratefulness.org. Accessed June 24, 2022. gratefulness.org/resource /expressing-gratitude.

Newmark, Amy, and Deborah Norville. *Chicken Soup for the Soul: The Power of Gratitude; 101 Stories about How Being Thankful Can Change Your Life*. Chicken Soup for the Soul, 2016.

Oppland, Mike. "13 Most Popular Gratitude Exercises & Activities." Positive Psychology. April 28, 2017. positivepsychology.com /gratitude-exercises.

Singer, Michael A. *The Untethered Soul: The Journey Beyond Yourself*. Oakland, CA: New Harbinger Publications, 2013.